Moderately Difficult

Great Things

He

Has Done!

Songs of Praise for Piano Four-hands

Mark Hayes

Editor: Larry Shackley
Music Engraving: Linda Taylor
Cover Design: Patti Jeffers

ISBN: 978-1-4291-2817-9

A Lorenz Company • www.lorenz.com

Foreword

My sister, who is three years younger than me, and I both took piano lessons from the same teacher when we were children. One of my most fun and funniest memories was when we attempted to play four-hand piano duets together. We had a book of songs from the movie *The Sound of Music.* One of the particularly tough songs was *The Lonely Goatherd* because of all the quick repeated notes in the melody. No matter which one of us played the hard part, that person fell behind in tempo and our "ensemble" fell apart. We would get tickled and start laughing. I don't remember if we ever ended the song. That's my first memory of four-hand piano duets. I hope yours is or will be better.

There are so many great reasons to play duets. Ensemble playing teaches you to be sensitive to another person's interpretation. For student/teacher relationships, it's a great way to mentor and model good playing. It's "fun" fighting for space on the piano bench. Then there's that pesky question of who's going to pedal throughout the piece. I'm sure you'll come up with lots of great reasons to share the bench and the 88 keys with a good musical partner.

Enjoy this first book of duets—I plan to write more. Use these arrangements to bring people into God's presence through worship. You are multiplying the power of praise by two.

—Mark Hayes

Contents

Christians, We Have Met to Worship

3

Mark Hayes
Tune: **HOLY MANNA**
by William Moore

Duration: 2:50

LT

6

70/1806L-6

10

To God Be the Glory

Mark Hayes
Tune: **TO GOD BE THE GLORY**
by William H. Doane

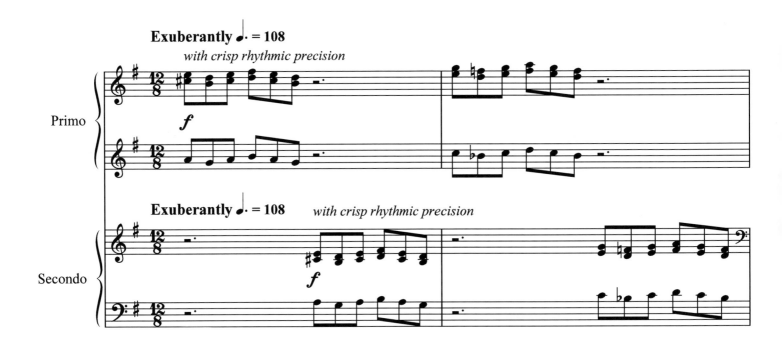

Duration: 2:55

My Jesus, I Love Thee

Mark Hayes
Tune: **GORDON**
by Adoniram J. Gordon

Duration: 3:40

www.lorenz.com

LT

Now Thank We All Our God

Mark Hayes
Tune: **NUN DANKET**
by Johann Crüger

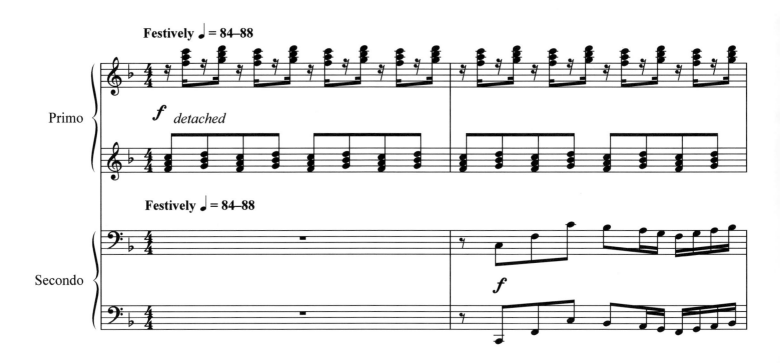

Duration: 3:45

LT

36

70/1806L-36

There Is a Fountain

Mark Hayes
Tune: **CLEANSING FOUNTAIN**
Traditional American melody

Duration: 3:40

LT

42

44

70/1806L-44

This Little Light of Mine

Mark Hayes
Music attributed to Harry Dixon Loes

Duration: 2:45

70/1806L-46

LT